My Little Book of

Manatees

By Hope Irvin Marston
Illustrated by Stephanie Mirocha

muddy boots™

Guilford, Connecticut

The giant gray manatee circled the warm spring waters of a Florida river. Round and round she swam.

>squeak!< >squeak!< >squeak!<

She thrashed her flat tail and poked her nostrils above the water. She took a few quick breaths.

SHOO-OOF! AAH-SHOO!

Then she continued circling.

That night her calf was born. He looked like a giant sausage. He was nearly as long as a baseball bat and weighed about sixty pounds.

The newborn manatee swam close to his mother. He flapped his paddle-shaped tail *up* and *down*. His flippers *wiggled* from side to side. Up he floated to the surface. He needed to fill his lungs with air.

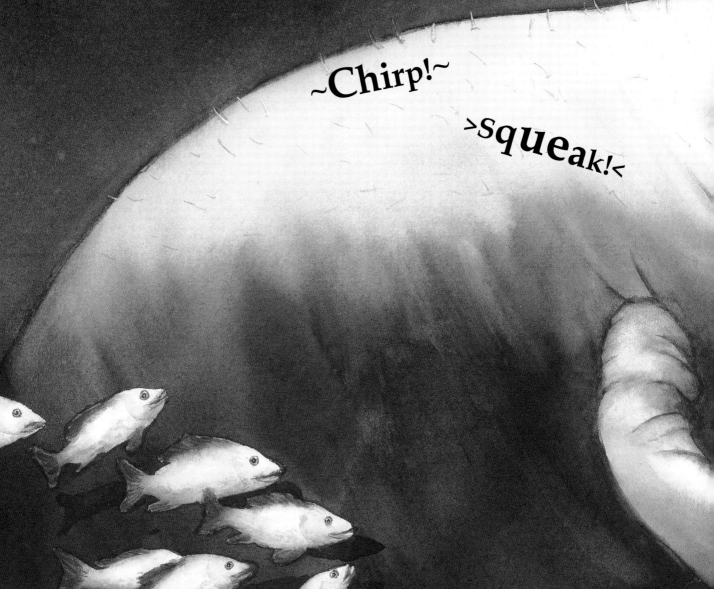

The manatee calf turned his body to look for his mother. His little blue eyes were the size of dimes. They opened like a camera lens.

His mother nuzzled him with her whiskery snout. She swam close to him.

~Chirp!~

>squeak!<

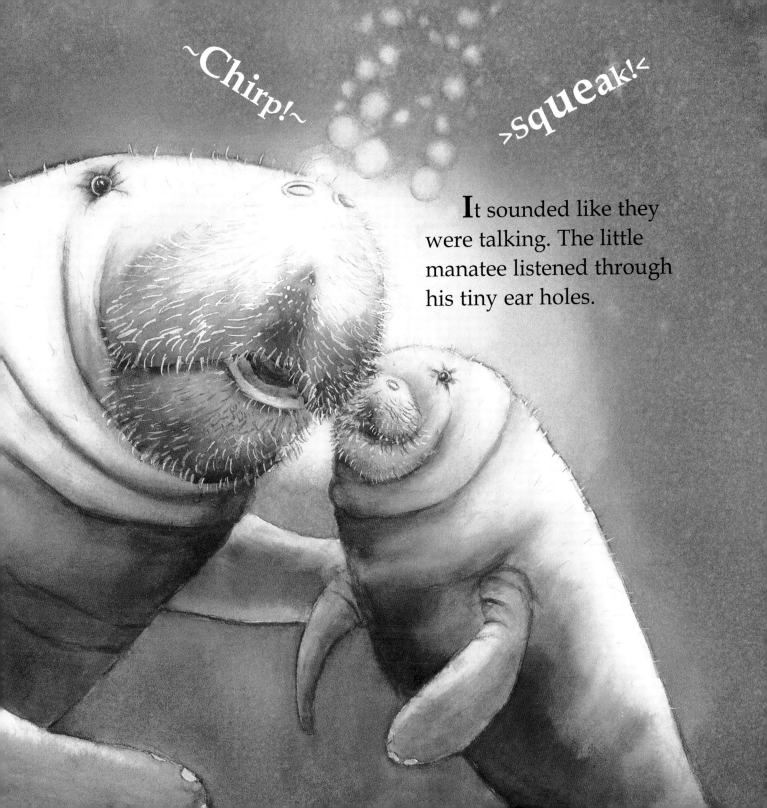

~Chirp!~

>squeak!<

It sounded like they were talking. The little manatee listened through his tiny ear holes.

The hungry baby searched for one of his
mother's thumb-sized nipples behind
her front flipper. When he found it,
he began to nurse.

His mother rose to
the surface to breathe.
The calf hung on.

The baby manatee finished nursing. He and his mother rested in the water. Their muzzles touched the sandy bottom. After a very short nap, the manatees floated to the surface.

FLIP! FLIP.

Their nostrils opened. The manatees breathed out. They breathed in. Then they closed the flaps on their nostrils and sank to the bottom of the river.

The manatees steered their bodies with their flippers. Sometimes they found objects like fishhooks or plastic can holders in the water. They shoved them toward their whiskers and mouthed them. Luckily, they did not swallow.

One day the calf caught a flipper in a piece of nylon fishing line. He p-u-l-l-e-d and *twisted* to get loose. The line tightened. The young manatee gave one more tug.

SWISH!

His flipper was free.

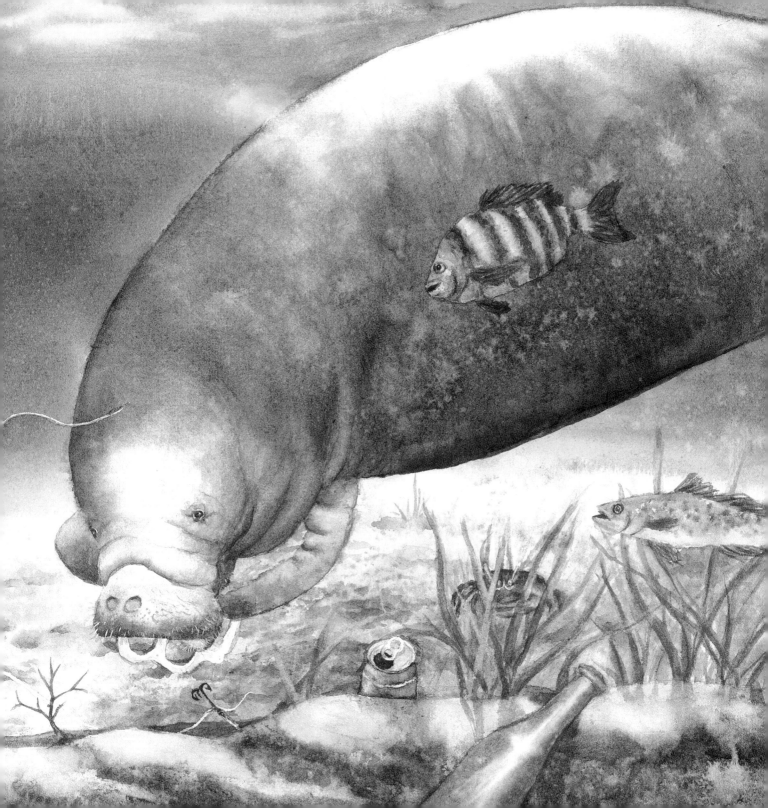

During his first year, the manatee calf nursed when he was hungry. His mother searched for water plants. She pulled them toward her mouth with her flippers.

MUNCH!

MUNCH!

Her huge teeth looked like crinkle-cut french fries. She chewed very fast. Every day she chomped down one hundred pounds of plants.

The mother manatee stayed close to her baby.
She taught him how to take care of himself.

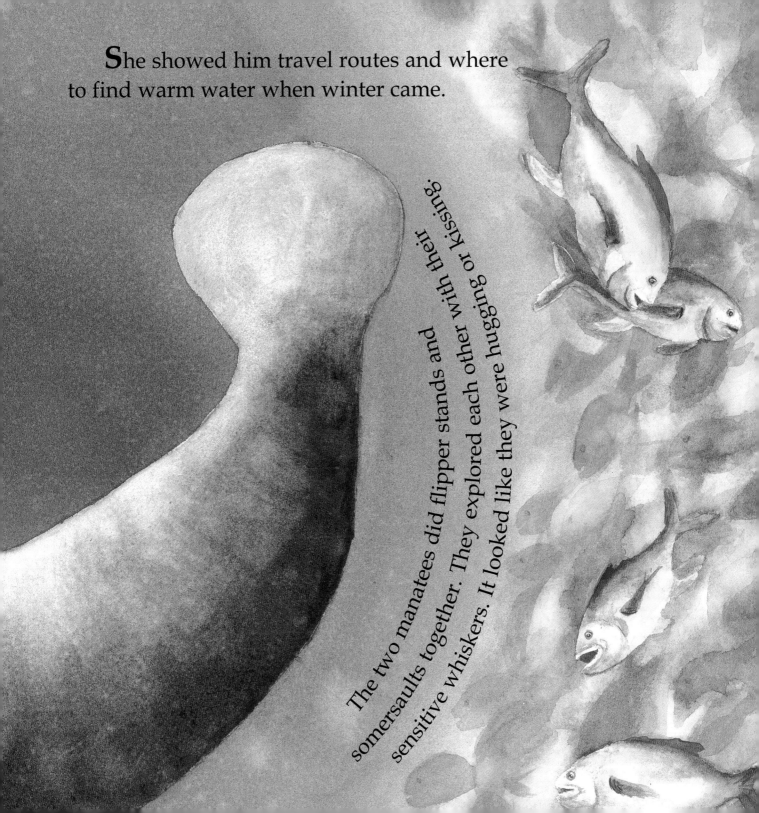

She showed him travel routes and where to find warm water when winter came.

The two manatees did flipper stands and somersaults together. They explored each other with their sensitive whiskers. It looked like they were hugging or kissing.

The manatees swam near the shore.
They stayed close to the surface.

The calf grew more teeth. He began to eat turtle grass. The sand in his food wore down his teeth. One fell out. Then a new tooth started to grow forward from the back of his jaw.

One morning the young manatee was eating water hyacinths. A speedboat zoomed toward him and his mother. His mother weighed a thousand pounds and she moved very slowly.

The whirring blades slashed through her thick skin, cutting into her back.

The water swirled above her as the boat sped on. When the water touched the wounds, the bleeding stopped.

The injured manatee rose to the surface to breathe. Her calf swam with her to safety near the shore. It would take many months for her deep wounds to heal. The jagged scars on her back would never go away.

Winter came. The water turned cold. The baby manatee and his mother headed to warmer water near the power plant.

They rode the strong currents together.

The manatees breathed together. They dived together. They turned at the same time.

They bumped and ((shoved))

They rolled over like barrels.

They played follow-the-leader.

And they swam upside down.

Spring came and the cold river warmed up. The manatees returned from the power plant where they had spent the winter.

When the calf was about two years old, he left his mother. He would live in the river until the water turned cold. Then he would swim back to the power plant with the others.

One day, several bull manatees began to follow the young manatee's mother. After trailing her for two miles, they caught up with her.

A year later her new baby was born. He flapped his paddle-shaped tail up and down. His flippers wiggled from side to side. He poked his nostrils above the water.

SHOO-OOF! AAH-SHOO!

He breathed in his first breath of air.
Then he dropped back into the water
to find his mother.

DEDICATIONS:

FOR ALYSSA, KASEY, AND KYLE
— H.I.M.

FOR ERLING AND SONIA
— S.M.

we jump in puddles

An imprint of The Rowman & Littlefield Publishing Group, Inc.
4501 Forbes Blvd., Ste. 200
Lanham, MD 20706
www.rowman.com

Distributed by NATIONAL BOOK NETWORK

British Library Cataloguing in Publication Information available

Library of Congress Cataloging-in-Publication Data available

ISBN 978-1-63076-376-3 (paper : alk. paper)
ISBN 978-1-4930-6217-1 (electronic)

♾™ The paper used in this publication meets the minimum requirements
of American National Standard for Information Sciences—Permanence of
Paper for Printed Library Materials, ANSI/NISO Z39.48-1992.

ACKNOWLEDGMENTS:

The author acknowledges the support of
the Save the Manatee Club and the Ask
Shuma Team at Sea World for fielding her
many questions about manatees.

The author wishes to thank Daniel K. Odell,
Ph.D, Senior Research Biologist, Hubbs-
Sea World Research Institute, for checking
the text for accuracy and completeness.